Shape Tracing and Practice

Tip:

You can get even more shape tracing practice by creating reusable sheets!

1. Take this book apart. Rip off the cover to more easily tear out its pages.
2. Place individual sheets into sheet protectors.
3. Write on the sheets with dry-erase markers.
4. Wipe off the marker to reuse.

Circle

Semicircle

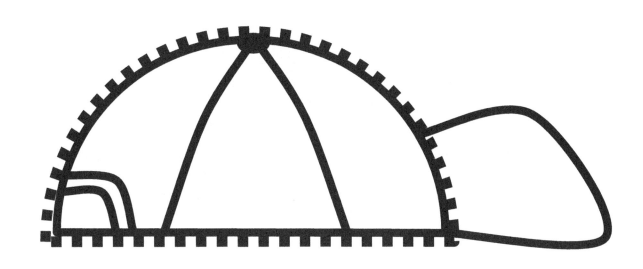

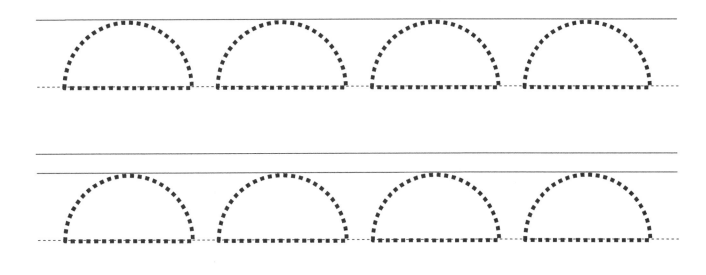

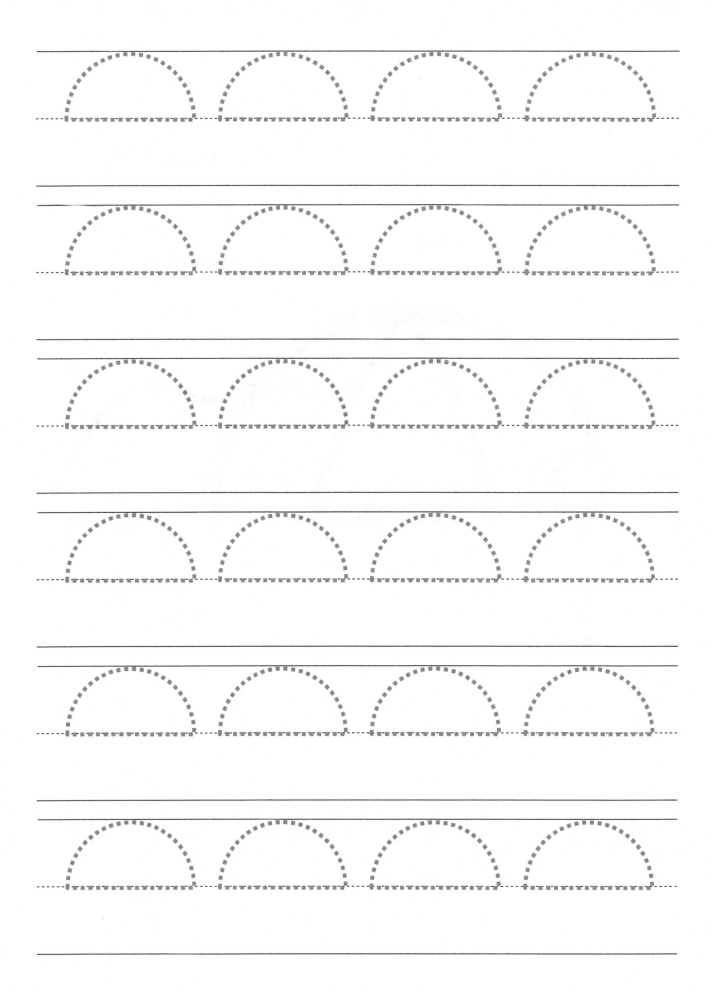

Oval

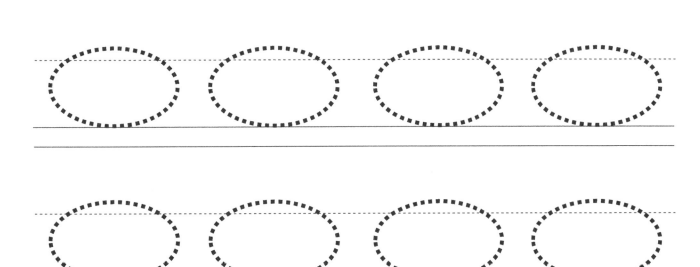

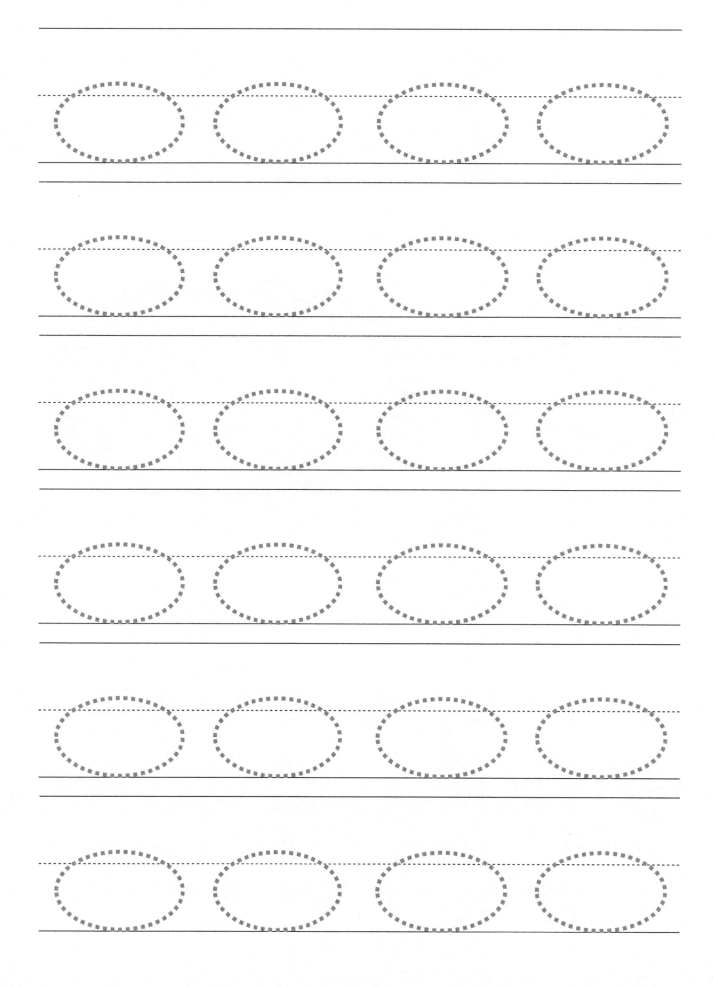

Triangle

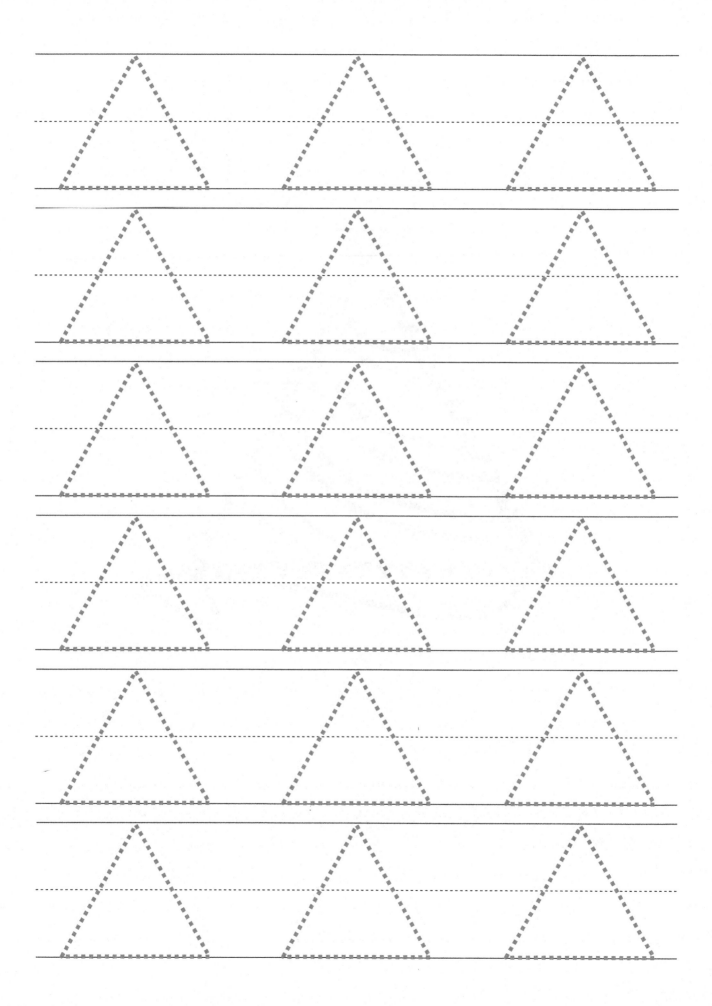

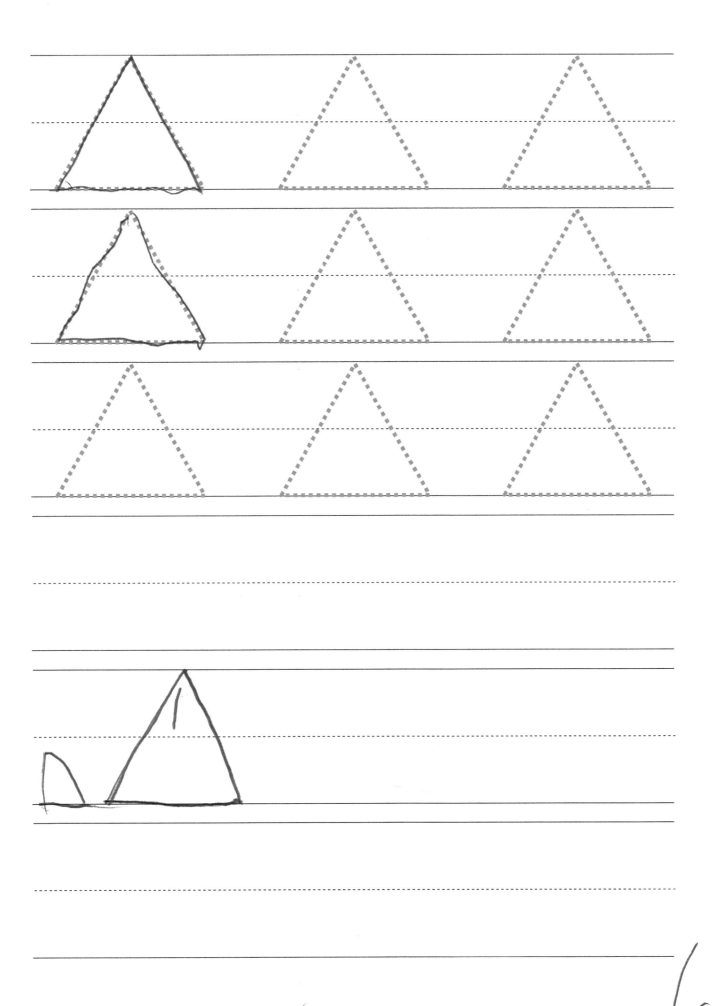

Square

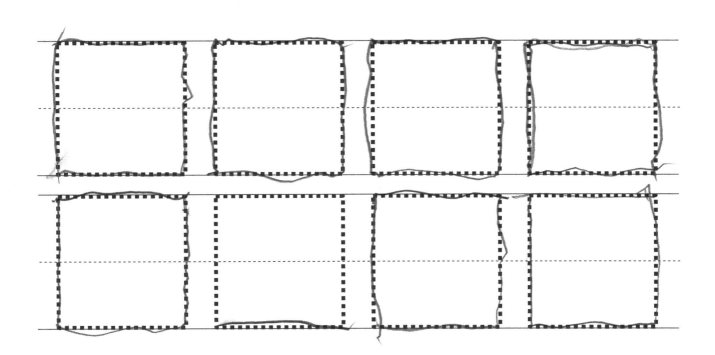

Rectangle

Parallelogram

ERASE

Rhombus

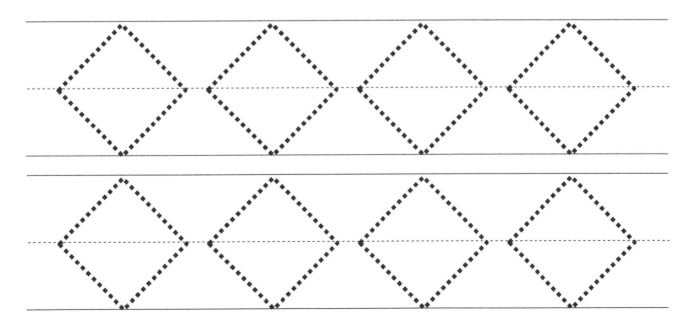

Trapezoid

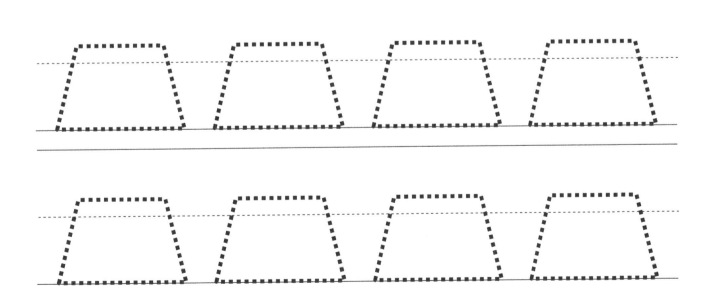

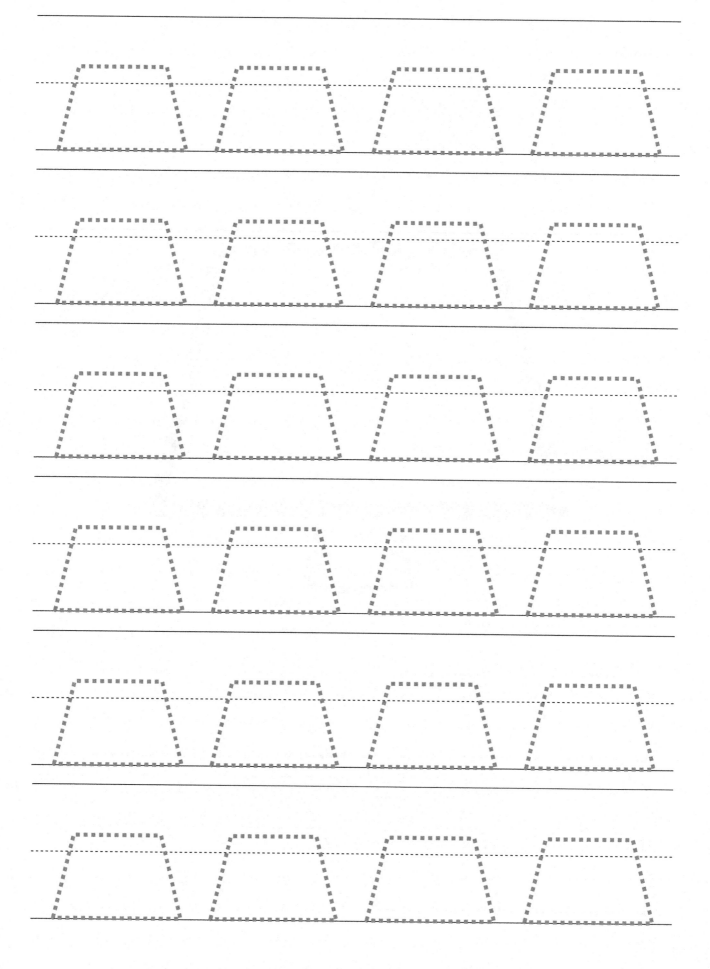

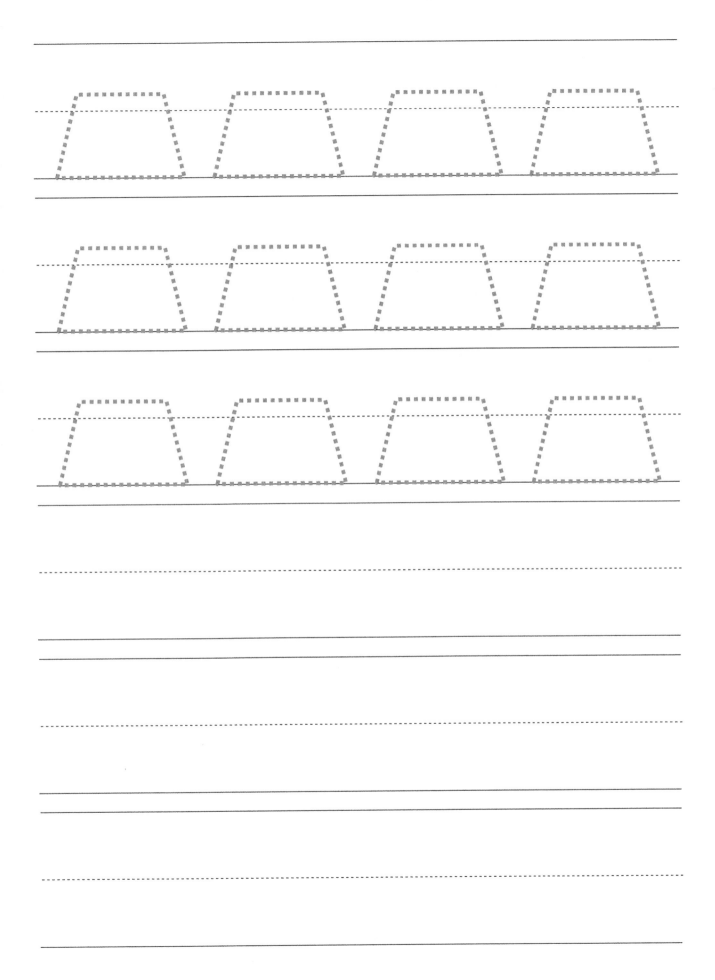

Pentagon

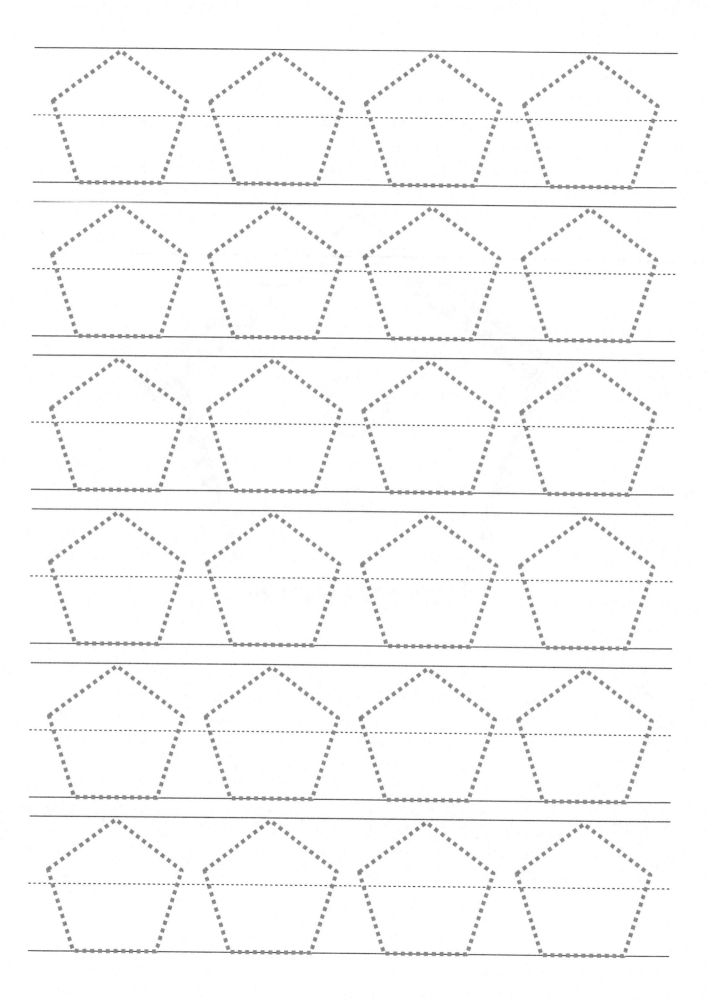

Hexagon

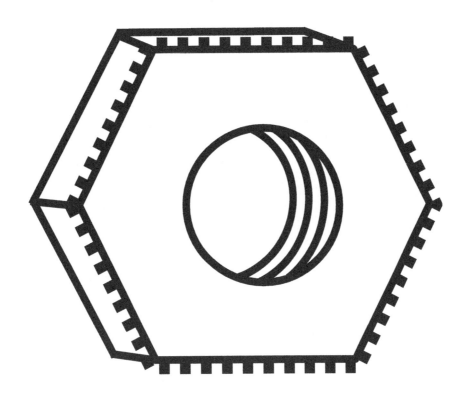

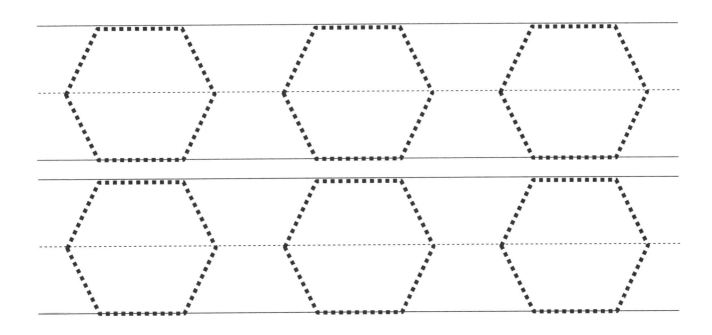

Decagon

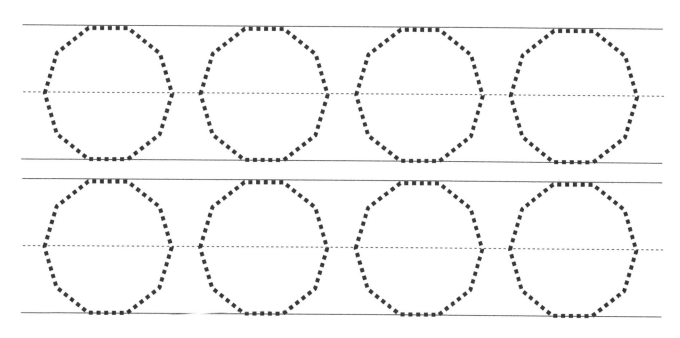

Dear parents and teachers,

Thank you for your purchase of this workbook. I know that there are many to choose from and I very much appreciate your decision to invest in this one.

I hope you and your children have found it useful and helpful. If you could spare a moment, please write a short review on Amazon about your experience.

If you would like to share feedback or comments with me directly, I would love to hear from you. Feel free to email me at sharon.sherry@outlook.com.

Take care,
Sharon

61814568R00030

Made in the USA
Columbia, SC
26 June 2019